The Rigid Body

The Rigid Body

Poems

Gabriel Spera

The Ashland Poetry Press
Ashland University
Ashland, Ohio 44805

Printed in the United States of America

ISBN: 978-0-912592-92-3

LCCN: 2012941194

Cover image by Gregory Muenzen

Acknowledgements

Some of these poems first appeared in the following publications:

Able Muse, "Bread and Fish"
Beloit Poetry Journal, "Romas"
Carolina Quarterly, "At the Medical Waxworks in Bologna"
Cavalier, "Mutability," "Ode to a Dentist's Drill," "Sumo," "Twins,"
    "Words, Words, Words"
Cave Wall, "Body Worlds"
Cimarron Review, "Masterful"
Dogwood, "The Bargain," "Cabbageworm"
Great River Review, "The Hopeless Ends," "Uniform Supply"
Hampden-Sydney Poetry Review, "Behold," "The Goose in the
    Bottle," "Wonderful"
Harpur Palate, "The Community," "The Forsaken Cry"
Kestrel, "Enough"
Missouri Review, "Studies for a Portrait"
Nimrod, "Apricots"
Prairie Schooner, "And It Begins," "Atlas"
Roger, "Grubbing," "The Hive"
Zone 3, "An Explanation," "Opossum," "The Pantry Moths in the
    Pheromone Trap"

Grateful acknowledgement is made to the National Endowment of
the Arts for supporting this project.

Thanks also to the Anderson Center for Interdisciplinary Studies in
Red Wing, Minnesota.

Immense thanks, also, to Natasha Trethewey for selecting this
manuscript for the Richard Snyder Prize.

ART WORKS.
arts.gov

Contents

IV. Hostages to Fortune

For R—, P—, R—, & P—,
hostages to fortune

I.

A Blind, Irresistible Urge

Apricots

It's wrong, I know, shameful to resent
the tree's unstinting act of giving, but
I've had all I can take of this sweet glut,
which will not wait for hands, but must, decadent,

flump to the ground with its zither of meddling flies.
For something in my pennywise heart can't let
gold go to waste, but bids me grab all the delicate
ingots I can hold, as I warily rise

on toddling ladder feet. What one life lacks
is another's nuisance. And what does it portend,
this epic crop? Has an old tree, sensing its end,
thrown all its failing strength to stay the axe

of time? Or has nature always tried to cram
her largesse down our throats, deaf to any voice
that dare say no? There was a time I could rejoice
in rot. It's too familiar now. And so I'll jam

and jar until the sweet stench stains my pores
and cupboards all but buckle to contain
too much to spread before June comes again
with more bright gifts than one heart can endure.

Decorator Crab

A drab pebble, a flecked shell, a shard
of olive-colored glass—the commonest things
can make him stronger, duller, harder
to discern. He is obsessed, like the sea itself,
with the world's miscrafted and abject,
and what he can't consume, he builds
into the scaffold of his back, the fauve
mosaic of his body's squat dome.
He has made a landscape
of himself, an island that sidles,
like desire, on infinite tangents.
And like the tourist who absorbs the local
dialect and dress, he draws no notice
as he picks from one cathedral
to the next, collecting knick-knacks
and paperweights to strand upon
his shelf. And though such luggage,
such tacky souvenirs, grow hefty,
harder to uphold, his stick-figure legs
and mitten hands will neither buckle
nor protest, but carry on, as ever
he must, too poor to walk away from all
he's hauled this far, too wise to chase
the luxury of a life unadorned,
the wealth of a forgettable past.
If he lives at all, it is simply
that he grasps the tidal line between shell
and façade, artifice and edifice,
being and not being perceived.

Cabbageworm

Blind hungerer, probing immanence of glut,
she'd raze the whole damn yard if given
half the chance, seasoning the dirt
with tight green peppercorns of dung. The lush
nasturtium leaves, just yesterday offered up
like soft communion wafers dyed
the minted green of all that fills our hearts
with darkness, now recall a child's first stab
at paper snowflakes, perfect forms debased
by graceless passage into fact. One thing is clear:
whoever promised us dominion over all
the beasts of earth has yet to clear it with
the bugs. Last fall, for instance, bowing
to snip the bounty of a summer's worth
of providence and mulch, what did I find
but a cabbageworm like this one,
lolling in a blur of flagrant marigold,
beading the corolla with her orange-tinted
excrement, her body, too, fluorescing, green
no longer as she built into herself
the glory of the petals she consumed
as though to show how what we hunger after
can't help but change us, stain us from within,
and that for every form and grace
there is a worm through which it passes,
given time, greedy enough to swallow
any flame, and every sun, and all
who turn their perfect hunger toward the light.

Opossum

Having seen the cubs, no bigger than a child's
first sneaker, ply the compost heap
for melon scalps and black banana peels,

who would not choose to believe this stiff
but bloodless heap, a puddle's width
from the curb, were simply feigning death,

might suddenly yawn, stretch out her cramped
hind legs, unkink the lanyard of her tail
and just start waddling down the walkway,

as she did most midnights, poking
her coffee-filter nose beneath the bugles
of calla lilies, rooting for cutworms

and snails like beefy teamsters plowing
roads of moony glister over
terra-cotta pots. And seeing the zipper

of her smile, who would not suspect
some impish prank, some childish game
of make-believe, for what could amuse

the dead enough to forget their own
undoing? On any other face, such a grin
might be received as the look of someone

suckerpunched by life too many times
to ever expect a happy ending,
or the look of peace that comes to one

at last let go from the crosshairs of a world
that begrudged enough for even
the most monkish to rummage a life from.

On her lips, though, it seems simply a smirk,
a sneer, that mocks the vast rest of us,
who've convinced ourselves we must—even

knowing all we know—somehow go on,
sidestepping the heap of our bloodless faith,
our stiff convictions littering the road.

An Explanation

Because the blood and lymph systems
in his species are conjoined, the male bedbug

has dispensed with mating dances
and vaginal copulation as costly luxuries

the most reviled of human parasites
can ill afford. Instead, he simply locks

the weaker female in a choke hold
and drives the rigid shim of his penis

deep into her belly, infecting her
with his pent-up seed. Evolution

has graced her with a callus
at the likeliest site of penetration

but this does nothing to repel
his surgical embrace

or render the moment of commission
any less painful or abject but at least

she doesn't hemorrhage to death.
No. She drags her brutalized body

to a crevice in the bedframe or the wall
and squeezes out there unattended

her motherlode of eggs, which soon enough
slit open, the hatchlings fanning out

in all directions, seething with a brute
thirst for blood they do not question

and can't explain, though it defines them,
and enslaves them, and consumes them.

The Hive

Something must've died, I figured, judging
by the orgy of fat black flies
that smudged the air. But no, they weren't flies,
but bees—a rogue swarm had set up shop
inside the fusebox, derelict
since the switch to cleaner breakers.
I edged nearer, like a hiker
toward a precipice, skin galvanized
by the hum of them, charging unimpeded
through the slot made by the warped door's
failure to meet the jamb. They drilled past me
by the dozen, coursing out and back
like cells in unseen vessels, carrying
grain by grain the sun's boundlessness
to their hive's dark heart, secreting there
the alchemized light. Then at once
the air shredded with the shrapnel
of alarm as the whole hive erupted
into frenzy, provoked, no doubt,
by news of a neighbor's fence
frothed with honeysuckle. But though they fumed,
a cloud chaos, a juggled puzzle, still
I beat the urge to bolt, but backed off slow,
my limbs near fossilized by the imminence
of attack, the winged pursuit of jolting furies
whose ire I had aroused. I made my break,
unscathed, but not unnerved, and slipped inside
to make a call to pest control,
keeping my distance till dusk locked down
the factory of their menace.
Mercifully, I never saw the sprays and dusts
they must've used, but came home only
to a pale invoice shimmed

beneath my door and out back, the fusebox,
like a crime scene, flung full open,
the five long combs, butter-colored,
hanging like dried cod or lungs, no longer
swelled with the ache of industry, tumored
with the few odd drones that hadn't
dropped off, unborn or out foraging
when the vapors went to work. And seeing
the spent shells of the others, flocking the ground,
they must've sensed how their hours now
were numbered, but seemingly didn't need,
though I hovered near, to stitch their vengeance
into whatever hapless body
happened past, to go down stinging, as I
surely would, settling the score with a world
too weak in soul to let them be.

Mutability

This season's flu, more popular than fear,
had filled my nose past brimming. Always I hear
a distant ringing in my punch-drunk head,
as I huddle with the clicker, too drugged to read,
stiff as anything flattened in the road
last week. A shivering kettle, a sweating toad,
my body's gone insane, and won't be told
to be at peace, to stop concocting green-gold
clams of phlegm, or spots on my tonsils like mold.
So, what exactly is this thing that's taken hold,
this virus, this chemical, leaching through a hole
too small to plug? Life at its purest, some say, its sole
purpose to continue, to insinuate some
part of itself in all that moves, to sow the same
division everywhere, greedy, like all who seek fame
to see its face on every surface, a face
that's changing, innovating, adapting, in fact,
even now, a protean protein, evolving so fast
it makes our heads spin, and the flu shot from last
year falls flat against the strain on this year's list,
stranger to our antibodies, cloaked in the mist
of sneeze and cough. Like all subversives, it must
trust in brief encounters, and in this, we're most
obliging, flailing for the subway post,
filching the teller's pen because we've lost
our own, crowding cramped pews to ease our lust
for pomp and ritual. How long would a virus last
without our plump, creased palms to smuggle it past
our bodies' guards, unyielding at their post?
It wants us all, but as with any pest,
consumption can't be absolute—the best
result's a restive occupation. For if it bent
every nucleus to its will, if its genes went

through every cell, what then? Getting all you want
can be a dead end, a clapped jaw you can't
gnaw free from. The shape of all we are was cast
in the forge of stress and selection, though in this case,
the flu's both shaper and shaped: those that came
with too much fire died in lonely hosts; too tame,
and they never found one. Life loves the middle, but time,
like the man who has everything, will soon tire
of common things, and consign them to the fire
of endless possibility. And all our fine
self-regard seems naïve when intellect can find
no edge over a thing devoid of mind,
a cellular weed harnessing an ill wind
to scatter its bitter seeds. And all our wild
faith in humanity, faith that a greater will
compels us, cups us in hand to keep us well,
our talk of throngs in heaven, outcasts in hell,
must please this virus, which wants hands to be held,
wants us to embrace without shame, to hold
our souls wide open, to fill with compassion the hole
of our hearts, to let our arms grow heavy with hope.

Actaeon

They're killing me, who gave them home and name—
clawing my haunches, clinging to my neck,
hurling their flawless forms in pure attack,
too crazed to see the grief beneath the game.

Even I no longer know my face,
the man I was—a dream they've shaken me
awake from with their brash cacophony,
mocked by my failing will, my fallen grace.

They'll pick my carcass clean, these hearts that hound me.
But then, who hasn't had his chest torn wide
by what he loves, or suffered to see his pride
unleashed? My strange, my useless hands confound me,

my head tossed in its thicket, my mouth gone dumb.
Too much a man—my crime and my defense—
unable to unsee what eyes have sensed,
unbe this broken beast that I've become.

The Pantry Moths in the Pheromone Trap

You almost feel sorry for the hapless bastards—
chaff-colored wings plastered to the tacky

yellow walls of the cardstock tent, tormented
by the musk, the siren scent, of the one

they can't help writhing even now to embrace,
too soused with lust to face the truth, the hard lie,

of her existence—proof again, it is a rare soul
who is not wedded to a fiction, or who

has not found himself held back from all he wants
by his own damned wings. Still, it's unnerving

to see firsthand the flawless way life baits
its killing jar with what we most desire,

the flame we can't help hurl ourselves against
and against. If only their offspring could resist

the earthy paradise of our cupboards, the unsealed
sacks and packaged meals, we might endure

their moony trysts, their midnight assignations.
But they know no bounds, those bone-colored grubs,

fouling and webbing the sifted and the ground,
turning our hearts and hands against them, condemning

the reformed, the born again, for crimes long past,
for sins they've lost the stomach to commit.

II.

Like Ghostly Apparitions

My Last Day as an Altar Boy

The doors and stained-glass transoms all flung wide
and still the air won't budge. In the swelter
and chafe of my stiff cassock, I kneel beside
the altar with a fistful of bells, like a butler
ready to call the dinner guests inside.

The congregation fidgets, widely spaced
throughout the pews, avoiding, like a mortal sin,
all contact, every mother's flushed face
fanned by an accordion-folded bulletin
sponsored by Day's bakery and Divine Grace

funeral parlor. And as the priest, by no means thin,
bends to kiss the altar, the crisp white linen
receives the sheen of sweat that buffs his skin,
darkening like a modern shroud of Turin.
The stale incense, candle soot, drone of the organ

tug my lids like window shades, my mind
drifting from the drowsy monotone and out
the doors, past the garden sprinklers realigned
to bless the bare bodies of the undevout,
to school—because the girl I sit behind

has found the trapdoor to my fantasies
and meets me there, her speechless lips and soft
gaze stirring in me something all these "thees"
and "thous" can't wholly smother. He holds aloft
a pale full moon. "Take this, for this is my body."

Arugula

A better gardener would've tilled them under—
the buckshot offspring of last season's tidy crops
that bolted in the summer's rough embrace.
I can't, humbled by the faith, the utter surety,
of those bitter greens that cast their hapless seeds
to spawn a tapestry of leaves they'd never see—
much the way you strewed the seeds of our regret
upon the raked beds of desire and went away
before the stirrings could take root. They bloomed,
despite my willful neglect, in blossoms pale and delicate
as any silence held too long. I kept them, pressed them
in the pages of my heart's dear diary in hopes
you'd one day thumb the binding wide and find
love's frail design for us, bared upon each blank sheet.

Exit Left

His glass drained, Steve rose, like a child just learning
to falter, and tottered toward the john. But the doorway
dodged him, and he strode face-first into the jamb.
He staggered back, like a movie zombie, shot
but not stopped. We tried not to stare—hadn't he earned
a few drinks? We knew more than he told, how weeks

before the wedding, his fiancée had started running
with a broker down the street, so what was to say?
Chin up? You're better off? Some see a door start to slam
and somehow slip through before the lock clicks shut.
Some flee their lives like a house on fire, only to find
the doors have been moved, the exits walled with bricks.

The Hopeless Ends

Someone who loved me let a pet store clerk
put a spider on her palm, a leggy
bonbon, a shy confection—the bitter
chocolate of its fur, the creamy brindling
of its knees. She didn't flinch, although it
ambled up her arm, but told me only
that it tickled, and walked soft. He plucked it,
a dark orchid, from her elbow's pale sleeve
and tried to hand it next to me, smiling
like a dentist to assure me that it
had no reason to bite, but I for one
had walked far enough through the world of men
to know that it really didn't need one—
pain was a reason in itself. And as
with all of life's uniquely offered gifts,
I held myself wise in that rejection,
that refusal to be drawn in. Only
now, years after, still shamed by the utter
emptiness of my hands, do I see how
fragile it was—how could I not grasp it?—
having since learned firsthand the hopeless ends
love drives us to. To think I didn't think
I was unworthy of her gaze, didn't
shrink from it, as it rose to me from her
outstretched palm and all it suffered to bear
for my sake. It's with me still, that spider,
crouched beneath the trapdoor of my heart.

The Work of Love
for Greg and Leslie

Give a poet the chance to speak of love and he'll
      take all night to spout his epic. Ask of marriage, and he'll
give you little more than a wry haiku.
      Take Shakespeare, for instance: How many plays
give marriage a flattering role? How many end with lovers who
      take their own unconsummated lives? In youth, we learn: love
gives the soul a heady taste of the sublime; marriage
      takes its socks off and leaves them on the floor. Love
gives rings, marriage begets toasters. But
      take it from one who knows (and believe me, I've
given this some thought): Marriage is like art—what seems easy
      takes effort, and what seems hard asks only that you
give it enough time. A poem like this, for instance, might
      take months to get right, yet it will seem I didn't
give it a second thought. In life, as in art, we can
      take comfort in knowing that sometimes fortune
gives more than we're worthy of. And through the journey that's
      taken you here, you've no doubt noticed people
give nothing so generously as advice. And though you should
      take it with a diamond-sized grain of salt, I'd like to
give you some of my own all-purpose admonition. First,
      take nothing for granted. Be like the toddler who
gives each freckle on your nose a shriek of wonder, and who
      takes her shoes around the house lofted like a trophy.
Give thought to how meanly time treats maker and made and
      take pride in nothing that can be passed from hand to hand.
Give no heed to the inklings of colleagues and critics,
      take council with none but the objective dead.
Give even these words their due measure of neglect, but
      take as gospel the least grunts of love. And while you can,
give as though you had everything and
      take as though you had everything. Because you will, I

give you my word, find joy provides all a body needs if
      taken in large doses. And joy comes like breath to those who
give what love takes, like song to those who
      take what love gives.

Enough

The sun comes out, as though it hadn't been gone
for years, and wouldn't go down again
for years. You take your sweater off, and turn
your face right toward it, bearing no ill will,
no resentment for the dark, the mortifying cold.
You embrace it like you embrace your mother
at the front door when she arrives, unexpected,
years after you watched her casket drop
into the earth. Love can be shrewd that way,
calculating, giving just enough warmth. Just enough.

Studies for a Portrait

1.
Consider her ability to sleep:
in cars on any errand lasting more
than two or three short miles; at home, slunk deep
in warm chenille, unable to endure

her dreary soaps; in bed, still lumped in sheets
until I've finished my commute and join
the workday world; past supper, when the heat
of wine weighs down upon her lids like coins;

midnight, when I strain saucer-eyed to hear
again that thingful sound that repossessed
my dreams, obsessed with what is always there,
the hands of men and clocks that know no rest.

2.
Consider her ability to eat:
soft gobs of guacamole scooped on chips
too small to bear; Dutch chocolate bars, not sweet,
but dark and coffee-bitter; lavish strips

of toro slivered over rice; a mound
of ice cream when nostalgia weaves its pall
about the house; a dish of pasta found
leftover from a meal no one recalls;

Korean beef, warm juk; red-curried Thai squid;
the noodles that she slurped when I first met her;
the thing she didn't cook but watched as I did
explaining how to cook it even better.

3.
Consider her ability to talk:
to halls filled with the skeptical nods of those
who would discredit her; about the stack
of papers on her desk that grows and grows and grows;

a blue streak to her sister in a time zone
twice removed; a filibuster to a stranger
stuck in line; in condescending tones
to certain ones who've managed to estrange her;

to nobody all day, penned up at home,
squinting at her screen till pixels double;
to me, although I'm in another room,
and strain for more than mrph and zazz and garbl.

4.
Consider her ability to want:
an easy job that pays more than mine does;
the dish I've ordered in a restaurant
that makes her own look bland; a chest of clothes

to pack and unpack as the seasons turn;
home in a city where the temperature
stays constant all year round; the gift she spurned
just yesterday, but suddenly adores;

not to be busy, but to have a task;
not to be famous, but to be respected;
not to be married, but to have been asked;
not to have kids, but to have not objected.

5.
Consider her ability to not
remember: whether or not she took her pill
this morning; where on earth could she have put
those figs; what happened to the water bill

she never paid; the punch line to the joke
she's badly telling; lyrics to a song
that's overplayed; the saucepan, belching smoke,
she set a flame to as the cordless rang;

the ending to a film she truly doubts
she's ever seen; the woman's name she met
last night; that silly thing we fought about;
that little thing we swore we'd both forget.

6.
Consider her ability to hate:
the squirrel gnawing half an apricot
still ambering in our tree; the angry wait
at table for a colleague who forgot

their luncheon meeting; being the last or first
guests to arrive; small people with small minds;
a government that panders to the worst
and richest elements; the rush-hour grind

when every street downtown's a parking lot;
a call from Dad that spoils her perfect plan;
me, when I remind her that I'm not
divine, but trip through darkness, just a man.

7.
Consider her ability to love:
herself, and how she looks in her black dress,
the slinky one; an argument that proves
my theory wrong; the backyard in distress

of hollyhock and dahlia run amok;
a list of things with all but three or two
crossed off; the fat lasagna that I make
on certain holidays; her mother, who

deserved a better life, a better lover
to live it with; me, though I least deserve,
and rise each day expecting to discover
all bleak, all black, all gone, my universe.

Sonnet (With Children)

My love is like a deep and placid lake...
Not now, sweetie, Daddy's busy, OK?
OK: my love's a deep and peaceful lake...
Here, Daddy can fix it. All better. Now go play.
Um, my love, yes—a rose that blooms in spring...
You tell her Daddy says she has to share.
My love's... My love's a lake that blooms—no, that springs...
On the wall?! Her what?! No, wait—I'll be right there.
OK—love, lake, spring, joy, flower bedding...
And why is the house so quiet now, I wonder?
Ah, fuck it! (Whoops! Don't say that!) You know where I'm heading.
Don't touch a thing—I need to get the plunger!
Forgive me, love, but time, as you know, is ticking.
So here: no you, no joy, no life. No kidding.

III.

The Most Impossible of Conclusions

And It Begins

The inconceivable finds its vehicle
into being, into fact: Fiat Punto—
Let there be an end. And it begins, a flash,
an airquake, a self-devouring chaos of
black plumes gloried with the halo of fireshine
and buckshot of cloudlight, thick chiaroscuro
thinning scrimlike as it spreads to let base shapes
at last condense, confused, from the debris sleet
and sand fall—the warped ellipse of steering wheel
and wheel drum, skewed rhombus of hatchback, diamond
shims of tempered glass, the skitting helix of
strut coil, flung rods and cylinders, bent, dented,
of drive shaft and shock, the colors dust-paled but
strengthening, spectral, spanning red to black as
moment starts to follow moment, the margins
stirring with the first coughs of lung rust, raw forms
with hands and feet bellying from the blood muck
and clay of those without, toward nothing certain,
leaking low sounds and bleats answered by others,
upright, eyestung, earclapped, edging toward oil soot
and crater, car, carcass, stunned by their newfound
nakedness in the face of all they've made, all
they cared for, having no word in the language
they woke up with for this new beast, this blind drive
toward ending that would devour them inside out.

The Forsaken Cry

About torture, they were all wrong,
the old masters, how little they understood
its tactics and procedures, how it takes place
as the world turns its innocent gaze on the wings
falling flaming from the sky, and how always
just a headline away are those who don't specially
want to know what's happening—the water, the cold,
the cramped kennels, the body checks, the terminals
clamped to bloody ears, the power drill
driving toward the strapped-down thigh.

In Dante's *Inferno*, for instance: the damned
are poked and lashed by batnosed fiends
who exhibit none of the delicate tidiness of those
who take their orders only from the highest circles,
and seem to forget that they who have let go
all hope of even the most inventive death
have no incentive to speak—assuming intel
is the goal—and any words retched up by a man
chin-deep in a fen of human excrement
must be taken for what they are: mere poetry,
inadmissible in all but the courts
of the bull-horned and dog-toothed,
and any witness, having followed his convictions
this far, though unaware the ground he trusts
lies upside down, yet knows he will never
return to the world of light.

Dark Night

At last the cuffs were loosened from my hands
and the gunny sack lifted from my eyes—
and still I couldn't see. I tried to stand
but struck my head, the cell too small, a cage the size

of a dog's cramped kennel—lightless, cold, locked.
For hours—gunfire, helicopters, the muffled thud
of falling mortars. I hunched against the cinderblocks
and waited, steeled, until sleep, like a cresting flood,

pulled me under. A slap of cold water from a pail
kicked me from one dark dream to another.
I was brought to a holding tank, huge as the provincial
passport office, packed with men restless to know whether

their bribes had reached the right palms. The door clanked
behind me, drawing their skittish gaze. The air
was brutal, animal, from the bare toilets ranked
along one wall, and the smell of cramped bodies, sour

and suffusive. A few who knew me came to greet me,
like rain out of season, but when we tried to kneel
and pray, we were pulled out, whipped repeatedly,
and made to squat and stand in time to the squeal

of a whistle. I blacked out, drowning in my hood,
and came to on the cold slab floor of the holding tank,
legs throbbing like phantom limbs. I pissed blood
for three days after. Sometimes, the water to the sink

would be cut for days on end so no one could bathe.
The rashes and dysentery were worse than nightsticks
and chains. Sometimes, we were marched in groups and made
to stand like new recruits while one of us, picked

at random, was jabbed with cattle prods. One kid,
scarcely older than my own eldest son, was hauled
across a bench and raped three times. No one dared
look away, let alone try to stop it. It was all

we could do to make believe we hadn't seen, pretend
we'd been blindfolded, deaf. That night, he tore
the feedwires from a hotplate, clutched the live ends
in his fists, and flicked the switch. He was dead before

we could stop him. No one gathered the body—it lay still
untouched the next morning. Some nights, I was dragged out
to a bare room, cuffed to a heavy chair, and grilled
about things I couldn't know or even lie about

convincingly. Some nights, I was left there, wrists ducktaped
to my ankles arced behind my back. Sometimes, I was shown
photos of my wife and told she'd been raped
by ten men, or would be, depending. I don't know

what to believe or expect except the worst,
don't know why I'm still alive, or how, if ever,
I'll fall back into the life I called my own, my universe
shrunken and boxed by pain. And always, I wonder:

the man they mistook me for, the one whose face
or name resembled mine—what crime did he commit
to make them want to tear his soul from its place,
and what could they have done to drive him to it?

Wonderful

Lymphoma, he rasps, almost proudly, heading off
the questions he assumes I'm too ashamed to ask,
having heard, no doubt, the rumors from the mothers
dropping kids off at the bus stop these past few months.
We're in a cramped auditorium, heated well
past comfort, clocking the start of the holiday
pageant our daughters have been giddy for all week.
He takes his Dodgers cap to fan his pasty throat
revealing a patch of scalp oddly suggestive
of a gray whale's scarred and mottled hide. The chemo,
he says, was almost too successful, in a sense—
took out the nodule in his lung, then set to work
on the vessels that fed it, etching them open
till they poured out, literally, his heart, and he
half-drowned in his own welling blood. Mercifully,
the children file in before I'm pressed to offer
some hopeful and inadequate reply, and take
their places on the risers, beaming as the room
coughs and settles. Then at once, they start singing—no,
shouting—miles from any melody, it's the most
wonderful time of the year. And as if on cue,
his toe starts tapping, his head bobbing, and his mouth
blossoms into song, the hap happiest season
of all, as though he couldn't hear his own pinched voice,
or didn't care that the rest of us could, having
surrendered his body to the joy peculiar
to those who've managed not to drop their brittle faith
in the improbable, who still rise the darkest
morning of the year fully expecting to find
the wide world boxed in mystery, and with each breath
a dazzle of shimmering gifts beneath a tree.

Uniform Supply

Corey's voice trailed off, the conversation bushwhacked
anytime they'd venture in, his eyes magnetized,
shadowing them through the store, maybe hoping they'd
steal some socks to prove the world still worked
the way it had to for his dicey tightrope walk
of normalcy. Ten years at least since his last tour
and still he couldn't trust them, couldn't fail
to draw a bead on them. Nor did he distinguish
the Vietnamese from anyone else who might
resemble them. Eating sandwiches in the stockroom,
a box canyon of teetering stacks of boots
and shelves of steel-blue work shirts, it was hard to tell
did he really not want to talk, or was he
milking every word? Either way, Joe, the owner's son,
sat rapt, like a dog beside the dinner table
who knows he won't be satisfied but won't be
kicked away with no bone. Joe wanted
to have been there, to have survived the acknowledged
hell of it, seen combat firsthand in the botched
paradise of the world, something his father
never did and wouldn't have the right to say
shit about, even if—or especially if—it meant
coming home a little damaged, like Corey, who
always left you feeling lucky if he walked away
from an argument you didn't realize you were having.
Even knowing what he knew, what the whole
world knew, he wanted to be part of it—not
to be a hero, if there even was such a thing, but
to have that horror to keep tucked in his pocket
like a note from the doctor that would excuse him
from the rest of his life, or a ticket to the skids
of failed potential that was stuffed into his fist
and not paid for with his own stale inheritance.

The Community

Someone heard a car pull up the drive,
so they hurried her out the back door
and through the woods to an abandoned
trailer home. And there it continued.
No lights, but dusk was still hours away
even in late Autumn. The carcass
of a burned-out toaster oven filled
the counter, and a Christmas tree, still
tinseled, stood tilted in a corner.
The smell of cigarettes and decay
rose from the cushionless couch as trucks
whined down the featureless interstate
nearby. Some boys left, others came, one
at least for each of her eleven
small years on earth. One flipped a cellphone
and started filming, compelled, no doubt,
by the same vague sense of history,
of moment, that moves the young soldier
told of the enemy's surrender
to shove a piece of the bombed-out mosque
into his pants. The community
voiced shock and regret when the details
were made public, when those that could paid
the bailbonds and slunk home and the news
rippled out, and did not, not at first,
blame the girl, the child of Mexicans,
for dressing like a high-school senior,
for wearing lipstick and blushing as
the car door swung wide, for sliding in
and ruining the lives of all their boys
who were just kids, after all, and who,
being black in a town known only
for its prison and refinery,

would always bear the burden of proof.
There were meetings—at the church, school gym,
clasped hands, tears, scripture, a microphone.
Somebody asked where was the mother?
Someone nodded, someone nudged, and soon
everyone was asking the same thing—
not, not asking, just saying because
really, did they need to ask, was there
really anyone who didn't know?

Masterful

Though it's a city job, Carlos isn't wearing
his orange vest and yellow hardhat,
but clomps around in tan ranchero hat
and washed-out denim shirt. The foreman
warns him once again, as he must, and Carlos
swears he won't forget again tomorrow.
He straps himself in to the motor grader,
skims a glove across the fat black knobs,
and eases forth with a mule-driver's patience,
leveling truck-dumped piles of raw fill
smoother than the sea of Cortez.
Maybe it's a gift, such effortless grace,
such seamless union of man and machine,
and maybe it's a sign how every morning,
punctual as the lunch truck with its
shave-and-a-haircut horn, he kills the engine,
clambers down, struts up close to a massive
chevron-treaded tire and just starts peeing,
as though the whole site weren't naked
as a soccer field, boxed along three sides
by green glass towers. Not that it matters—
the soil he darkens will be asphalted over
soon enough, and even now, here comes
the water-tank truck, spewing like a fire plug
wrenched open in the mid-city heat.
Small hot-pink pennants still mark
the heavy conduit we sank just yesterday,
and we've got planks on edge, framing
where the walkway's going to be.
The cement mixer inches up, its great drum
putting like a clock hand teasing toward the hour.
And Hector levers the crusty sluice above
the ready beds, the newsprint-colored mortar

plopping like horseshit to the ground,
where Manny makes quick work of it, his trowel
and squeegee broom drawing it so tight,
a dropped dime would roll to a standing stop
and never topple over. There is a thin line
between miracle and mastery. Even
Carlos stands, hat off with the rest of us,
nodding as with subtle understanding.

Sisyphus

Again
I wake
and already I
can't do it, can't
go on. But then, there
I am, dragging my way through
the same dead rituals, breaking my back
for no reasons I can comprehend, my best
days receding wildly. Every ounce of me aches, every
sprocket in my body missing teeth, my soul and bones
steadily losing ground to the constant drag of gravity and time.
Still, I persist, dogged by the fact that I've accomplished nothing: despite
all my sacrifice, the howls of the disconsolate, the suffering of the damned
continue as they have and will forever. I've lowered my sights—I'm too old
to move mountains—and still it's never enough, on any given day, the one rock
that most needs moving goes unmoved, as all my plans get crushed between the rock
of my body's dwindling strength and the hard place of the world's age-old
indifference. If only I could escape this rut, get beyond this one damned
hump, I'm sure my whole world would settle into place. So, despite
each day's identical failure, I keep slapping clean my palms, time
and again. Because something in my vain, deceitful, or bone-
headed heart blinds me to the fact that every
tomorrow will be exactly like today, at best,
assures me there's no sense turning back,
no choice but push on through.
Still, most nights, lying there
in bed, I can't
help hoping I
won't wake
again.

Bread and Fish

The call comes during the bouillabaisse—
lobster claws, clams, shrimp, mussels, and rock
cod schooling in a broth of homemade stock,
wine, tomato, garlic and bay, and just a trace
of saffron. His mother, three time zones away,
was dead, in a Medicare-funded room the dismal
green of key-lime pie, the settled-in smell
of lilies and sterile gauze. I'd been cooking for days,
the feast of Christmas eve, the longest day
for children and sinners alike, bickering in my head
with my father, who always overcooked the squid
and couldn't bear to watch me set my cleaver edge right
down the middle of each lobster's wriggling chest
to kill it. Gone, the woman who, despite all, refused
to leave the home he grew up in, cluttered, confused,
the gutters split, the porch off-kilter, depressed
by years of snow. He seized his chance, when she went
into the hospital, to clear it out—threw wide the shades
and set about dismantling piece by piece the decayed
architecture of her decline, wrecking the tenement
of books and papers stacked up on the sagging
mattress too packed to sleep on, defusing the firetrap
of grimed appliances junked on the countertop,
sweeping tchotchkes from the shelves and bagging
the toys plucked from some neighbor's curb. It was all fresh,
the fish, nothing frozen, though of course the dried
cod, the baccalà, had to soak inside
a pot of cold water three whole days before the flesh
could reconstitute, lustrous as a prayed-for
messiah. Arrangements would be made, but for now
it was fine for the hospital staff to follow
whatever were the standard procedures.
A silence, which I break, suggesting we postpone

the rest of dinner, but he won't hear of it.
Perhaps, in clearing her things, he'd prepared for it,
the news—or knowing that nothing now could be done
felt a pent-up hunger, a vaguely hollow mood.
I poured more wine—it was already decanted—
and sliced more bread for whoever might've wanted,
and tried to keep our focus on the food.
Our empty shells piled up—the hammer-cracked
claws and shale-black mussels, the clams that clicked
open like pocket watches compulsively checked,
as though to mark a watershed, the exact
moment of their predictable defeat. We'd had our fill
of what the evening offered, but couldn't stop
dabbing our bread crusts in the broth to sop it up,
double-checking that we'd scraped out every shell.

Romas

"Kill these yellow jackets," he says, gesturing
to the winged shards of flint and gold converging
on the edge of the folding table all but
buckling beneath the weight of squat mason jars
and stockpots brimming with parboiled tomatoes.
He hand-cranks the sieve that squeezes pulp into
a bowl and sheds the rinds like a molting snake.
His bare arms, like an army surgeon's, are mucked
to the elbows, the gray threads on his chest now
stark and coarse against the backdrop of skin gone
hazel in the unshirted hours spent tending
the heat-breathing vines, staking, twining, pinching
the rampant shoots. In one hand, he lifts a green
sweating bottle to his lips, while the other
readies a dishrag to smack a syndicate
of insects vindictive as a frayed lamp wire.
"Damn these wasps," he says, flicking the dazed and dead
with his slotted spoon. He tops off one more jar
and screws the lid-ring with a sound like tires
on gravel far away, and holds it aloft
to let the sunlight fuse through it, transform it
to something molten, pulsing, like the heartflow
of Vesuvius, or a blood-oil pressed from
twenty suns to grease the engine of the day.
"That's gonna be good," he says, gently nodding
his satisfaction before setting it down
with the ranks already marshaled on a bench.
He drains his bottle, still sweating, and towels
the bright gore from his hands. "Someday when I'm gone,"
he says, like someone who understands at last
the dry wisdom of advice he didn't heed,
"you'll remember me with all these pots and jars,
up to my chin in fresh tomatoes, swatting
these damned yellow jackets like some kind of fool."

The Desert Blooms

Graced by a season rainier than anyone alive
remembers, the California desert has come alive
in colors more vibrant than anyone who sees them
will probably see again. They drive to see them,
an hour or so outside the city, the state park
thronged by hundreds with the same idea, the line to park
long as a stalled freight train. He opens her door, extends a hand
to ease her out. She steadies herself, right hand
on his arm, left on her four-footed cane, and they walk
at a problem's pace along the narrow paved walk
that ribbons past the nature center, through low-slung hills
smothered in a dense slather of wildflowers, hills
like ocean swells slicked with sunset or an algal bloom—
orange poppies, topaz lupines, butter-yellow blooms
of cinquefoil, frail stalks bowing to let the wind
gallop through. And who would expect such wind—
loud as a helicopter with its searchlight trained
right outside the house, pitching them like a train
too packed to find a seat in. Each step is painful
though she tries to hide it, which makes it more painful,
frustrating, to watch, and all because he thought
it would do her some good to get out. He never thought
it would be so complicated, so difficult,
though as she'd say, *at my age, everything's difficult
and painful.* Not exactly a complaint—talking
about aches and illness, for the Irish, was like talking
about the weather, mere statement of fact. *What can't be cured
must be endured,* she'd say, *and there is no cure
for growing old.* It seemed simple enough, something
outside their routine that might give them something
bright to focus on. What could be more hopeful
than desert scrub resurrected in hues the most hopeful
would never dare dream? And after weeks of rain, what's more

47

affirming than a walk in the sun? But no more—
there's no point in going on. He should know nothing
ever works out the way he plans. Nothing.
They start back, still battling the wind, the long way
to the car, which, at this pace, looks hours away.
"I wish this damned wind would stop blowing,"
he mutters. *Ah, look at you, mad at the wind for blowing!*

Behold

That time again: small flocks
of piping birds shoot past my window
and over the gravel roof of the rundown
body shop next door. Without meaning, I fix
my gaze on one amid the shotgun burst
of wings, but it's no use—in a blink,
I've lost it in the scatter and bank
of twenty more exactly like the first.
Oh, omens, auguries—what are those years
I used to know by heart, each vivid minute
separate and distinct? A blank sky. In it,
black flecks converge, till no one soul there
can be perceived—only the flock, sojourning
briefly in the chase of a dwindling morning.

Ode to a Dentist's Drill

Mystical, how the light from the spot lamp
glints off your nib, the way candleflare
delights crystal, as you near my lips, plump
and blubbery with Novocain, cramped
with gauze wads and spit tube rasping for air.

Your one note, screech of fingernails on chalkboard,
transports me back to a childhood, wary
of all things offered as their own reward.
You do in minutes what would take the hordes
of tartar years of mining in my dark quarry,

grinding my grinders, mole in my molars—what
makes all my hard parts so prone to rot and wear?
No pain but in things, you say, but it's not
the pain, but the idea of it, the thought
that what I fail to feel will go too far,

will brush against the nerve you've unburied,
jolting me up and through your strict ablation
like a finger through the sewing needle's flurry.
We can't fear the unknown, but we can worry
disasters vivid in imagination.

I hear you, not through my ears, but in my head,
like the voice of god, the concentration camp
odor of smoking bone, the tang of blood
curdling nose and tongue, numb, but not dead,
my palms gone cold with dew, my jowls unclamped.

But yours is the Midas touch—through you, though poor,
I'm crowned, my jaw is steeled, my mettle's plain,

my grin made whole. You strip me to the core,
throw bare the rifts that must be filled with ore.
My mouth, thrown wide, receives the bread of pain.

Body Worlds

Unlike his sculpted form, the basketball
glued to his fingertips retains its skin
and color, while his surge from the pedestal
defies all instinct for self-preservation,
suspends him in a ribcage-cracking fall

beneath the backboard that he'll never bear
the brunt of—not as long as such tableaux
attract a paying crowd. From his lidless stare,
with its fixed gaze of curious surprise, we know
nothing of who he was or how he came here,

only that someone believed eternity
would be unthinkable, for him in any case,
if the body, with its threads of memories,
simply dissolved, like stacks of newsprint erased
by rain. Better that his body should be

timeless, a monument, a bust of Caesar
made of Caesar, a pharaoh gutted, drained,
and sewn up stuffed with frankincense and myrrh.
Better that his whole body should remain
rigid, scarlike, for that's what memory is—a scar

or ridge whose forming is relived each time
a fingertip or thought catches and slips
along its length like a kite string on a power line.
Without exception, when my fingertips
rediscover, beneath her bikini line, the fine

furrow, like the seam of a basketball, I'm back,
jarringly, inside the surgical suite,
the tubes and bags, the scrubs, the sleek black racks

of jittery diodes, as she lies there, hands and feet
strapped down, spread-eagle, the needle in her back

erasing everything below her neck
so casually, she smiles like a child asleep
while beyond the sterile drape, a hand selects
a scalpel from a tray and draws a deep
red rule, a fine equator that bisects

her belly's globe, without the briefest flinch
or pause, as though she were a mannequin,
or something human in the vaguest sense,
beyond all time and pain. He prods the skin
by the incision till the edges blanche

and pucker like a ball gashed in the mower,
then pulls into this world one flawless body,
bloated, coughing out its liquid slumber,
wailing as though air were purest agony
and light a titan greedy to consume her.

I scissor the cord, rubbery as squid,
while someone smears a salve across her eyes.
A brutal debut, and one that nobody should
have to relive. But at least she keeps her insides
inside—unlike her mother, profanely spread

across the table with a mophead of guts
and mottled vitals being fished out or stuffed
back in, the shoehorned oval of the cut
gaping till the doctor, having seen enough,
begins to stitch and glue and tape it all shut.

And here in the menagerie of plasticine
bodies and parts—the dancer boiled down to vessels
and nerves, the smoker's lungs clotted like the lint screen

on a dryer, the sprinter with his muscles
peeled back like the lid on a can of sardines—

who could help but picture himself arranged here
in a life-defining pose? And true, such a fate
offends our sense of self, but all we are
is what we've kept of what we've touched, which evaporates
without the clay of mind, the body's paper,

to hold it. I see it, marble-hard—my body,
aching toward them, desperate to believe
we could survive this flesh, yet keep what it carried.
But no—what survives us are the scars we leave
on the lives we'd give our lives to leave unbloodied.

IV.

Hostages to Fortune

Sumo

Such a figure must confound and torment
the shrewdest tailor. Better simply to go swaddled
in next to nothing, a loin cloth, a bath garment.
And forget shoes—that pendulous waddle

would defeat them. Even the flagstones seem depressed
by their near failure, and benches sulk
beneath those buttocks, exuberantly fleshed.
What fool would hurl his will against such bulk?

To try is to be rebuked, repulsed, mocked
as something trifling, a mere pinch, a penny's worth,
deluded to believe oneself a man of stock
and substance without such gravitas, such girth.

Will those limbs find rest in any spot?
Do they even build bedframes so vast, so strong?
How does one person grow so huge? Ah, but she's not
one person, now is she. Not quite. Not for long.

The Bargain

"Thou child of my right hand"

At times, I think it a fair-enough trade:
the errant finger that I did not crop
on the cutting board, the toe I didn't shred
beneath the mower, for the life that stopped
inside her. For surely, by that loss, we made
a reckoning that pleased some measured god.
He was our Isaac, taken in trust to pay
for tragedies that did not come, for joys
we took on loan. But that is not the way
she sees it, my one love, who'd gladly give an eye
or serve up bloodied hands if that would buy
or barter back the heart that came and did not stay.
All night, in darkness, drifting far from sleep,
she counts our fingers up like baby sheep.

At the Medical Waxworks in Bologna

The men, of course, never died during childbirth
and so were moved to study, maneuvering
scalpels down the body's prime meridian,
excavating the uterus like a jar
from an antique tomb. And that one's death might mean
deliverance for others—this was gospel,
after all—they cast the vital parts in wax
from thigh to ribcage, creating maps to lead
the doctor through the topography of death,
to teach his hands to draw each Lazarus from
the dark all life divides. Unlike their maker,
they've survived, these rendered effigies, despite
the fires of human history with all its
tendency toward naught. Displayed in glass caskets
like the pure, unrotting saints, they blur the line
between science and sideshow while suggesting
what makes us most human can never be fixed
in stone and what's most ugly inside us lasts
beyond the last mention of our names. The womb
in this casement, for instance, herniated,
tongue-colored, giving birth to its stillborn self.
Or here, another like a poorly thrown urn,
the walls too wet or too thin, collapsed inward,
a small hand thrust out as though grasping for air.
Or this one, bloated beside a fist-sized head
still clamped in gleaming tongs, the body fishboned
in the birth canal. And another, with child
half born, a cough shy of original sin,
a triple coil of pale umbilical cord
tendrilled around the neck. In their day, perhaps
they confirmed it's when we seek to prove free will,
to demonstrate agency over being
and not, that we reveal ourselves most fully

the hands of god's plan, for surely god, whose works
are perfect, and thus incapable of waste,
would never pour soul into any body
he knew would not be born into this world, though
surely no one has yet drawn breath upon Earth
without one. Now, with god quite gone, they simply
showcase what happens to a woman's body
when science gets through with it, how artfully
pain can be coaxed into shape, how life concocts
tortures worse than the mind of any jailor,
and how always it's the innocent and weak
who must suffer despite the best intentions
of those who should know better but still believe
some grace, some virtue, could come from human hands.

Mazatlan

What better place to make ourselves forget,
or nearly so, her empty womb—scraped out, reset
like a clock turned back to gain an hour of sleep.
The margaritas, made from scratch, were cheap
and packed a punch—the more so for our weeks
of fruitless abstinence. And though we didn't speak
a lick of Spanish, it didn't seem to matter—
the locals spoke English like us, maybe better.
The balcony of our mango-colored room, fourth floor,
looked out on a barren island just offshore.
A water taxi took us there for free,
or nearly so. We strolled, luxuriously,
amid the tidal pools in sun so bright
our shadows paled and hid beneath our feet. All night,
the moon, no longer new, gleamed in its ascent
like a scalpel edge unstitching the firmament.
Hands meshed, we watched the undulations spill
their pearls of foam, chalky in the overkill
of light cast from the hotel pool. And every crest
that tackled and withdrew seemed to suggest
in its hoarse stage whisper: Go, prepare the way
for those who will succeed. We packed and paid
and went for one last amble after breakfast
before the airport shuttle would come collect us.
We'd hardly gone two steps from the hotel gates
when a barefoot girl approached us, proffering kites
and wind chimes made from coconuts and shells.
We looked, unaware that local custom held
the day's first sale, if lost, would haunt the rest.
She trailed us, cutting the price till it was less
than we could bear. We bought a kite—how could
we not? The local scrip would be no good
back home, and the sky seemed needy, blue, depressed,
lost for something to hold against its chest.

Grubbing

The jay's up early, and attacks the lawn
with something of that fervor and despair
of one whose keys are not where they always are,
checking the same spots over and again
till something new or overlooked appears—
an armored pillbug, or a husk of grain.
He flits with it home, where his mate beds down,
her stern tail feathers jutting from the nest
like a spoon handle from a breakfast bowl.
The quickest lover's peck, and he's paroled
again to stalk the sodgrass, cockheaded, obsessed.
He must get something from his selfless work—
joy, or reprieve, or a satisfying sense
of obligation dutifully dispensed.
Unless, of course, he's just a bird, with beaks—
too many beaks—to fill, in no way possessed
of traits or demons humans might devise,
his dark not filled with could-have-beens and whys.

Twins

At their best, my eyes do not keep faith
with the utter singularity

of things and fail to resolve each line
from its visual stutter, its shy

comer-after, but for once I don't
need to look twice or twice as hard to

absorb the full weight of what I see:
two jitters across the CRT,

two fetal beeps tracking each swelling
contraction, in synch with my own heart

balled like a hand held breathless to mouth.
And as they crisscross across the screen,

the jagged plots are conjoined, compressed
by my sleep-bereaved eyes to what seems

a single inscription, possible
to decipher, but still elliptic

in meaning—like the signature note
in the doctor's firm hand: take two of

me in the morning, or the flawless
calligraphy darkening the walls

of the sultan's pale bedroom, declaring
in endlessly knotted arabesques:

there is no god but god is his name.

Words, Words, Words

We repeat ourselves and repeat ourselves
and trust our selfless work won't be in vain.
Night-night. Pee-pee. Bye-bye. No no no.
We know a word worth saying is worth
saying till it fills the smallest mouth
with helpless joy. There is an order
to be followed—every page in every book
must be reread the same way time
and time again, or else the world's vast pane
of certainty will break. *Again, again,*
she cries, happily, after every happily
ever after, as even I have cried
in unguarded moments, wishing that the joys
revealed in wayward flits of memory might be
lived again, with keener understanding.
Again, again, we cry, and if the storyline
grows wearisome to adult ears,
it's only that we've turned too many pages
in the fable-book of hope to not
suspect its simply better not to know
what happens next—although we always do,
we know how grief repeats itself,
how we ourselves repeat ourselves
in unexpected ways—as in the child
who gives us back the song we didn't know
we knew by heart, who plays dress-up in
the gestures and roles we've worn too long
to feel the heft and weave of, or who,
all on her own, picks up a book
and makes believe that she can read it, having
learned what all great stories have in common:
One day, she says, and slaps it shut, *The end.*
One day. The end. One day. The end. One day.

The Goose in the Bottle

She stands in the drizzle of her can's pink spout
as though she were the flowers she meant to water
while inches from her shoes, though teased with spatter,
the marigolds and cosmos remain in drought.
Still, they gamely spread their petals, as though to say,
"Carpe, carpe!" A poor choice of words, they soon discover,
as she tugs, with all the tenderness she can muster,
their wiry stems to make a limp bouquet.
No matter—the prospects for such blossoms, plucked or not,
are much the same. But now she's crammed into her can
through a hole too small for even her small hand
a flower, and can't get it out. She lifts the pot
to Daddy, who knows the secrets of all things puzzling—
doorknobs and nightlights, shoelaces and buttons—
and as he peers in, considering his options,
he recalls the story of the man who put a gosling
in a bottle. When it grew fat, he went to the temple
and asked how to get the goose out from inside
without killing it or breaking the glass. The abbot sighed.
"The problems we make for ourselves, however simple,
have no solutions." But that won't appease his daughter,
who won't be told her happiness does not require
a single blossom, or satisfy his own desire
to be divine. He takes the can and adds more water
until the flower head floats up to where his fingers
can snag it. Another tragedy averted,
a small faith in the world once more rewarded.
She stands, beneath his tutelary gaze, eager
to unpuzzle this bloom of nature's riddle,
plucking, like the feathers of a goose, its cryptic petals.

The Mad Scientist

Some days I want to unmake my creations,
start all over with a new set of parts—
new hands that won't heap heartache on frustration,
new mouths that won't deride my simplest thoughts.

Not that they're defective—quite the opposite.
They've grown into their lives in ways I never
dared dream, and show no flaw, no deficit
of grace. But they grow strange to me, and ever

less mine. They leap, and cringe when I recall
how once I laughed to see them try to stand
and fall, and rise again and again fall.
When was that moment they let go my hand

for good? Nothing now seems to need my help.
They wake, they wash, they tug their clothing on,
they fill their bowls and pour the milk themselves.
Then they leave. I'm a stopped clock while they're gone.

Hellions all, they hiss at me by day,
but call out in the night, their dim room haunted.
I come, and hush them back to sleep, and stay,
afraid to close the door on all I wanted.

It used to drive me mad to see them wreck
my instruments, my beakers and alembics,
pretending to be me absorbed in work,
perfecting every sigh (uncanny mimics!).

They take no interest in my interests now,
and I, too, feel uninspired, and unobsessed.

The demons that drove my grandest schemes have somehow
gone mum. I turned lead into gold—what's left?

And what did I expect—they'd do my bidding,
help me conquer the world? If anyone's
a vassal now, it's me—serving, or waiting
to serve, mazemaker thrown in his own dungeons.

Some days I would unmake them. But mostly I'm
too tired. Even the fullest life can become
a chore. And though I fooled death for a time,
in time I'll go to where I brought them from.

They'll miss me, but that won't bring me back again.
If nothing else, they will have learned life's full
of second chances, and sometimes worth the pain.
Just being here proves all things possible.

Atlas

My world has grown so small I can hardly bear it.
Tragic, to think what once these hands achieved,
the oceans overthrown, the mountains heaved,
the monster pinned and weeping that I might spare it.

These days, these hands know nothing but the numbing
sameness of work, the petty tasks that consume me.
Rigid, heavy, cold—would any who once knew me
recognize this stone that I'm becoming?

The day breaks and ends on the unremitting
wailing of the innocent. I'm powerless to end it
and helpless to endure. My heart, its dreams suspended,
has become a moon—dark-sided, scarred, forbidding.

Shoulder it long enough, and any weight
becomes the whole and name of who you are.
And if we falter before we get too far,
it's not that the burden we choose to bear is great,

it's that we grow so puny underneath.
It starts out simple enough—a shell, a stone,
small things you come to need, small lives you've grown
attached to. Then one day it's the length and breadth

of the sky itself you're trembling to support,
and not one star among the dazzle can you set down
without all the firmament crashing to the ground,
a galaxy of tears to fill your hands. What starts

in levity ends in gravity—any child could
teach us that. Take this. Hold it. Don't let it fall.

When did the simplest things become so impossible,
so pointless to even try? I thought I understood,

thought myself above it all, too strong
to falter, to fail. I got that backward, too.
I thought I could watch the measured days slip through
my hands and not feel bitter. I was wrong.

I thought I understood, but what's to know?
I tried to embrace the world. I really tried.
Some days, I weep to feel it all backslide
toward chaos. Because I can't hold on. And I can't let go.

The Richard Snyder Publication Series

This book is the fifteenth in a series honoring the memory of Richard Snyder (1925-1986), poet, fiction writer, playwright and longtime professor of English at Ashland University. Snyder served for fifteen years as English Department chair and was co-founder (in 1969) and co-editor of the Ashland Poetry Press. He was also co-founder of the Creative Writing major at the school, one of the first on the undergraduate level in the country. In selecting the manuscript for this book, the editors kept in mind Snyder's tenacious dedication to craftsmanship and thematic integrity.

Editor Deborah Fleming screened for the 2011 contest, and Natasha Trethewey judged.

Snyder Award Winners:
1997: Wendy Battin for *Little Apocalypse*
1998: David Ray for *Demons in the Diner*
1999: Philip Brady for *Weal*
2000: Jan Lee Ande for *Instructions for Walking on Water*
2001: Corrinne Clegg Hales for *Separate Escapes*
2002: Carol Barrett for *Calling in the Bones*
2003: Vern Rutsala for *The Moment's Equation*
2004: Christine Gelineau for *Remorseless Loyalty*
2005: Benjamin S. Grossberg for *Underwater Lengths in a Single Breath*
2006: Lorna Knowles Blake for *Permanent Address*
2007: Helen Pruitt Wallace for *Shimming the Glass House*
2008: Marc J. Sheehan for *Vengeful Hymns*
2009: Jason Schneiderman for *Striking Surface*
2010: Mary Makofske for *Traction*
2011: Gabriel Spera for *The Rigid Body*